The Talking Fish and Other Folktales

An Imprint of Unbound Script

ISBN : 978-93-92088-95-7

Published by **Unbound Script**
Plot No. G-20, Basement,
At Seven Wonders Business Centre,
B-10, G Block, Preet Vihar, Delhi, 110092
E-mail : books@unboundscript.com
Website : www.unboundscript.com

The Talking Fish & Other Folktales
Edited by Kamani Gayakwad

Price: ₹199/-

Printed in India

The Talking Fish and Other Folktales

the kid books

Preface

Hello little Friends! explore and enjoy with this book.

We specially created this book for you.

So you may enjoy and learn something from the stories. Beautiful illustrations are depicted to make the stories more interesting. It will teach you life lessons and the way to tackle with problems.

Hope our efforts and hardwork will help you to learn new things.

Beautiful illustrations are depicted to make the stories more interesting.

Contents

The Goldsmith

In the older days, ornaments were made to order. If anyone wanted to have an ornament made, he generally entrusted the quantity of gold required for making it with the goldsmith and after two, there of four days as the case may be, the goldsmith would make it and keep it ready according to specifications.

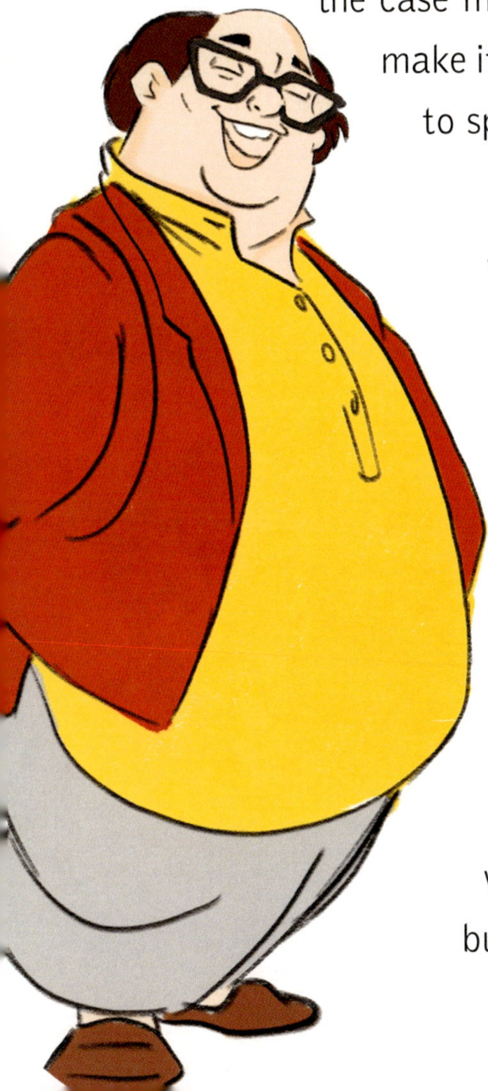

The goldsmith generally worked in his own, workshop. A rich zamindar wanted to have a necklace made for his daughter, who was about to get mamied. The best goldsmith in the locality was Chilean. So, he was asked to do the work. No doubt that Chilean was a good workman. The wriiten setence is correct but this one is more simple,

but it was well known that whenever he touched gold, a little of it would vanish under his palm. The zamindar didn't want this to happen, and so he asked one of his servants to stay in the Chilean's aala throughout the day. After the day's work, Chilean would leave the gold, in whatever state it was to the servant, who would weigh it and make sure that there was not the slightest loss.

In four day's time, the work was over. It was a beautiful necklace. The zamindar was eager to see it, and ordered it to be brought to his house. So it was taken to him in a piece of velvet, the goldsmith walking in front and the servant behind. On the way to zamindar's house they had to cross a small brook. When they came to the middle of the brook the necklace fell into the water. The goldsmith made

a hue and cry and jumped into the water. He however recovered it and both of them Straightaway went to the zamindar's house. The zamindar and his family. were immensely pleased to see the beautiful necklace which was exactly as they had wanted it to be. He gave a present to the goldsmith, besides the remuneration. The zamindar also thanked and congratulated his servant, who had watched over the work so well. But their joy did not last long. A week later it was found that the colour of the necklace had changed. No one knew how it happened. What actually happened was this. Chilean, the goldsmith cleverly made an exact replica of the necklace in brass.

This was done secretly in his house. He earlier kept the brass necklace in the middle of the brook. When the real necklace fell, it was not taken out; instead the brass necklace was brought out,while the golden one, remained in the brook. On his way back to his house he picked it up. And the one given to the zamindar was made of brass!

The Hidden Treasure

Once upon a time, there was an old farmer, who had four sons. The farmer's sons were now grown men who did not work. The farmer had a large piece of land where he grew his crops. However, the sons never showed any interest or will to start working and earning for their future. The old farmer was worried about his sons' future and what they would do once he died.

Soon, the old farmer fell very sick and was not expected to make it. He was on his deathbed and was worried about what his sons would do after he was gone. "I must come up with a plan to teach my sons a valuable lesson," the farmer thought.

On his deathbed, the old farmer calls all his sons to gather around him. "It's time for me to tell you a secret," the farmer said as his sons listened curiously. "There is a hidden treasure on the farmland which no one knows about!" he said.

The sons were surprised. "What? A treasure? Then why are we living like poor farmers?" they exclaimed. To this, the farmer replied, "It is not so easy to find that treasure, sons. Only the worthiest one will be able to find it."

The sons were deeply intrigued, but the treasure was too tempting. "How difficult can it be? Let us dig the entire farm and find it," they decided and started digging up the field. "It's sunset but we still haven't found even a trace of the treasure," they said as they ended the day very tired.

A man passing by heard the commotion and came by. "Hello, boys. I see you have dug up a very large farm there! You might as well take these seeds and plant them here," he suggested. The brothers did not like the advice but decided to do it anyway.

They planted seeds and went back home disappointed at not finding the treasure. However, their seeds soon grew into healthy crops. "Let's go sell these crops in the market," one of the sons suggested. At the market, they earned a lot of money for their healthy crops. Excited about the earnings, they started heading home, when one of the sons said, "Brothers, do you realise

that our father simply tricked us into digging the farm and planting seeds? There was never any treasure over there!" But as they thought about it some more, they realised something important. "Brothers, the treasure was not in the field, but we cultivated it with our hard work and sweat! Our crops and the earnings we made with our efforts is the treasure that our beloved father was talking about!"

They then realised that nothing came for free and that hard work was important and necessary to gain something. The brothers then overcome their laziness and start working hard for their future.

The white hare and Crocodile

Long, long ago, when all the animals could talk, there lived in the Kerla, a little white hare. His home was on the island of Oki, and just across the sea was the mainland of Kerla.

Now the hare wanted very much to cross over to Kerla. Day after day he would go out and sit on the shore and look longingly over the water in the direction of Kerla, and day after day he hoped to find some way of getting across.

One day as usual, the hare was standing on the beach, looking towards the mainland across the water, when he saw a great crocodile swimming near the island.

"This is very lucky!" thought the hare. "Now I shall be able to get my wish. I will ask the crocodile to carry me across the sea!"

But he was doubtful whether the crocodile would consent to do what wanted. So he thought instead of asking a favor he would try to get what he wanted by a trick.

So with a loud voice he called to the crocodile, and said:

"Oh, Mr. Crocodile, isn't it a lovely day?"

The crocodile, who had come out all by itself that day to enjoy the bright sunshine, was just beginning to feel a bit lonely when the hare's cheerful greeting broke the silence. The crocodile swam nearer the shore, very pleased to hear some one speak.

"I wonder who it was that spoke to me just now! Was it you, Mr. Hare? You must be very lonely all by yourself!"

"Oh, no, I am not at all lonely," said the hare, "but as it was such a fine day I came out here to enjoy myself. Won't you stop and play with me a little while?"

The crocodile came out of the sea and sat on the shore, and the two played together for some time. Then the hare said:

"Mr. Crocodile, you live in the sea and I live on this island, and we do not often meet, so I know very little about you. Tell me, do you think the number of your company is greater than mine?"

"Of course, there are more crocodiles than hares," answered the crocodile. "Can you not see that for yourself? You live on this small island, while I live in the sea, which spreads through all parts of the world, so if I call together all the crocodiles who dwell in the sea you hares will be as nothing compared to us!" The crocodile was very conceited.

The hare, who meant to play a trick on the crocodile, said:

"Do you think it possible for you to call up enough crocodiles to form a line from this island across the sea to Kerla?"

The crocodile thought for a moment and then answered:

"Of course, it is possible."

"Then do try," said the artful hare, "and I will count the number from here!"

The crocodile, who was very simple-minded, and who hadn't the least idea that the hare intended to play a trick on him, agreed to do what the hare asked, and said:

"Wait a little while I go back into the sea and call my company together!"

The crocodile plunged into the sea and was gone for some time. The hare, meanwhile, waited patiently on the shore. At last the crocodile appeared, bringing with him a large number of other crocodiles.

"Look, Mr. Hare!" said the crocodile, "it is nothing for my friends to form a line between here and Kerla. There are enough crocodiles to stretch from here even as far as China or India. Did you ever see so many crocodiles?"

Then the whole company of crocodiles arranged themselves in the water so as to form a bridge between the Island of Oki and the mainland of Kerla. When the hare saw the bridge of crocodiles, he said:

"How splendid! I did not believe this was possible. Now let me count you all! To do this, however, with your permission, I must walk over on your backs to the other side, so please be so good as not to move, or else I shall fall into the sea and be drowned!"

So the hare hopped off the island on to the strange bridge of crocodiles, counting as he jumped from one crocodile's back to the other:

"Please keep quite still, or I shall not be able to count. One, two, three, four, five, six, seven, eight, nine—"

Thus the cunning hare walked right across to the mainland of Kerla. Not content with getting his wish, he began to jeer at the crocodiles instead of thanking them, and said, as he leapt off the last one's back:

"Oh! You stupid crocodiles, now I have done with you!"

And he was just about to run away as fast as he could. But he did not escape so easily, for so soon as the crocodiles understood that this was a trick played upon them by the hare so as to enable him to cross the sea, and that the hare was now laughing at them for their stupidity, they became furiously angry and made up their minds to take revenge. So some of them ran after the hare and caught him. Then they all surrounded the poor little animal and pulled out all his fur. He cried out loudly and entreated them to spare him, but with each tuft of fur they pulled out they said:

"Serve you right!"

When the crocodiles had pulled out the last bit of fur, they threw the poor hare on the beach, and all swam away laughing at what they had done.

The hare was now in a pitiful plight, all his beautiful white fur had been pulled out, and his bare little body was quivering with pain and bleeding all over. He could hardly move, and all he could do was to lie on the beach quite helpless and weep over the misfortune that had befallen him. Notwithstanding that it was his own fault that had brought all this misery and suffering upon the white hare of Kerla, any one seeing the poor little creature could not help feeling sorry for him in his sad condition, for the crocodiles had been very cruel in their revenge.

Just at this time a number of men, who looked like King's sons, happened to pass by, and seeing the hare lying on the beach crying, stopped and asked what was the matter.

The hare lifted up his head from between his paws, and answered them, saying:

"I had a fight with some crocodiles, but I was beaten, and they pulled out all my fur and left me to suffer here—that is why I am crying."

Now one of these young men had a bad and spiteful disposition. But he feigned kindness, and said to the hare:

"I feel very sorry for you. If you will only try it, I know of a remedy which will cure your sore body. Go and bathe yourself in the sea, and then come and sit in the wind. This will make your fur grow again, and you will be just as you were before."

Then all the young men passed on. The hare was very pleased, thinking that he had found a cure. He went and bathed in the sea and then came out and sat where the wind could blow upon him.

But as the wind blew and dried him, his skin became drawn and hardened, and the salt increased the pain so much that he rolled on the sand in his agony and cried aloud.

Just then another King's son passed by, carrying a great bag on his back. He saw the hare, and stopped and asked why he was crying so loudly.

But the poor hare, remembering that he had been deceived by one very like the man who now spoke to him, did not answer, but continued to cry.

But this man had a kind heart, and looked at the hare very pityingly, and said:

"You poor thing! I see that your fur is all pulled out and that your skin is quite bare. Who can have treated you so cruelly?"

When the hare heard these kind words he felt very grateful to the man, and encouraged by his gentle manner the hare told him all that had befallen him. The little animal hid nothing from his friend.

The hare was overjoyed at his quick recovery, and kneeling down at his feet, said:

"I cannot express my thanks for all you have done for me! It is my earnest wish to do something for you in return. Please tell me who you are?"

"I am no King's son as you think me. I am a fairy, and my name is Lakshmi" answered the man, "and those beings who passed here before me are my brothers. They have heard of a beautiful Princess called Yakami who lives in this province of Kerla, and they are on their way to find her and to ask her to marry one of them. But on this expedition I am only an attendant, so I am walking behind them with this great big bag on my back."

The hare humbled himself before this great fairy Okuni-nushi-no-Mikoto, whom many in that part of the land worshiped as a god.

"Oh, I did not know that you were Okuni-nushi-no-Mikoto. How kind you have been to me! It is impossible to believe that that unkind fellow who sent me to bathe in the sea is one of your brothers. I am quite sure that the Princess, whom your brothers have gone to seek, will refuse to be the bride of any of them, and will prefer you for your goodness of heart. I am quite sure that you will win her heart without intending to do so, and she will ask to be your bride."

Okuni-nushi-no-Mikoto took no notice of what the hare said, but bidding the little animal goodby, went on his way quickly and soon overtook his brothers. He found them just entering the Princess's gate.

Just as the hare had said, the Princess could not be persuaded to become the bride of any of the brothers, but when she looked at the kind brother's face she went straight up to him and said:

"To you I give myself," and so they were married.

The Stag and His Horns

There was a beautiful forest and a clean lake in the middle. Animals used to come to this lake to quench their thirst. It was a common place where hunters also gathered to catch animals or kill them.

A stag arrived at the lake. The water was clean and calm. When he was about to drink water, he saw his pair of antlers. He was so proud and happy that he had such a beautiful set of horns. When he approached the water further, he saw his thin legs.

He was not happy with his ugly legs. They were skinny, and he considered them disgraceful. He thought about how his antlers could be so beautiful and his legs ugly. He despised the legs. He ignored his legs with pride and kept drinking water peacefully.

The hunters knew that this lake was a great place to find animals. They knew that they could score big if they reached the right time.

They moved closer to the lake with their dogs to track down animals. Suddenly, the stag heard the dogs barking and the hunters whispering. Sensing danger, the stag bounced from the water and started running to a safer place.

It created a splashing sound in the lake, and the dogs heard the stag running away. The hunters understood that their dogs had traced something. They unleashed the dogs to run after the stag.

The stag was at his best speed when his beautiful antlers caught in the lower branches of a tree. He was

stuck and could not even move a step further. He started struggling. The more he struggled, the more he got stuck in the branches.

He could hear the dogs coming closer every second. His heart started beating faster with fear, but his legs did not give up.

In The Stag and His Horns Picture Story, his legs pulled and pulled. The strength of his legs set the antlers free from the branches, and the stag started running for his life.

The dogs could not even glimpse the stag as his legs were super fast.

Miracle upon Miracle

In a certain place, there once lived a merchant by the name of Nanduka, and a merchant by the name of Lakschmana. The latter, who had lost all his wealth, decided to travel abroad. It is said that a person who has lived well in a particular place but stays there after losing their wealth is of common mind. Furthermore, a person who, reduced to misery, remains at a place where they were once happy is worthy of reproach.

In his house, there was a large set of heavy iron scales that had been acquired by his ancestors. He gave these to the guild-master, Nanduka, for safekeeping and set forth for foreign lands.After he had pursued his desires for a long time abroad, he returned to his homeland, and said to the guild-master Nanduka, "Guild-master, give me back the scales that I left here for safekeeping."

Nanduka replied, "Oh, your scales are no longer here. The mice ate them up."

When he heard this, Lakschmana said, "Well, Nanduka, if the mice ate them up, then it is through no fault of yours. That is the way of the world. Nothing in it is eternal. But now I would like to bathe myself in the river. Send your child with me, the boy named Dhanadeva, to carry my bathing things."

Nanduka, fearing Lakschama because of the theft he had committed against him, said to his son, "Child, your uncle Lakschmana wants to take a bath in the river. Go with him and carry his bathing things."

Yes, with truth they say: No one does a favor for another, unless driven by fear, greed, or some other purpose. And further: If someone shows you unusual courtesy, be cautious, lest it lead to a bad end.

Nanduka's son, carrying the bathing things, set forth happily with Lakschmana. After taking his bath, Lakschmana threw Nanduka's son Dhanadeva into a cave on the bank of the river, and sealed the opening with a large stone. Then he rushed back to Nanduka's house.

The merchant asked him, "Speak up, Lakschmana! Tell me, where is my child who went to the river with you?"

Lakschmana said, "He was taken away from the river's bank by a falcon."

The merchant cried, "You liar! How in the world can a falcon steal a boy? Give me back my son, or I will bring action against you at the king's court."

Lakschmana said, "Oh, you who always speak the truth! A falcon can carry away a boy, if mice can eat a large set of heavy iron scales. If you want your son back, then give me my scales!"

Thus quarreling one with another, they went to the king's gate, where Nanduka cried out loudly, "A dastardly crime has happened here! This thief has robbed me of my child!"

Hearing this, the judges said to Lakschmana, "Return the guild-master's son to him!"

Lakschmana answered, "What can I do? Before my very eyes a falcon carried him away from the bank of the river."

Hearing this, they said, "You do not tell the truth. How could a falcon be capable of carrying off a fifteen-year-old boy?"

Lakschmana answered, laughing, "Ha! Listen to this proverb: When mice can eat a thousand pounds of iron, then a falcon can carry away an elephant, to say nothing of a little boy."

The judges said, "What do you mean by that?" Then Lakschmana told the whole story about the scales. After hearing this, they laughed at what Nanduka and Lakschmana had done, reconciled the two with each other, and made them respectively return the scales and the boy

The Mongoose and The Child

Once upon a time in a village, there lived a Brahmin with his wife. One day, they were blessed with a son. The Brahmin thought to have a pet for the child so as to protect him as well as to get a companion for him. He went in search of the pet and found a mongoose. He brought him to his house.

At first, the Brahmin's wife was reluctant to have a mongoose as a pet.

But later she agreed to it. The mongoose and the child became close friends. Both, the Brahmin and his wife, started loving the mongoose like their own child. But the Brahmin's wife was always a little sceptical about the mongoose being near the child.

On a particular day, the Brahmin's wife had to go to the market to buy vegetables.

She told the Brahmin to take care of the child. The child was sleeping peacefully in the cradle. The Brahmin then left for begging alms. He thought that the mongoose would look after the child.

A few hours later, the Brahmin's wife returned and saw the mongoose at the door. His mouth was completely blood-stained. She inferred that the mongoose had killed the child. At once, she threw the basket of vegetables on the mongoose.

She ran towards the room in search of her child and to her surprise, saw the child still sleeping quietly in the cradle. But on the floor was a dead snake which was bitten into pieces.

Then she understood that to save the child, the mongoose attacked and killed the snake. Realizing her terrible mistake, she rushed back to the mongoose only to find him dead. The Brahmin's wife cried aloud as she had killed the loyal mongoose.

The Blinds and the Elephant

There were once six blind men who stood by the road-side every day, and begged from the people who passed. They had often heard of elephants, but they had never seen one; for, being blind, how could they?

It so happened one morning that an elephant was driven down the road where they stood. When they were told that the great beast was before them, they asked the driver to let him stop so that they might see him.

Of course they could not see him with their eyes; but they thought that by touching him they could learn just what kind of animal he was. The first one happened to

put his hand on the elephant's side. "Well, well!" he said, "now I know all about this beast. He is exactly like a wall."

The second felt only of the elephant's tusk. "My brother," he said, "you are mistaken.

He is not at all like a wall. He is round and smooth and sharp. He is more like a spear than anything else."

The third happened to take hold of the elephant's trunk. "Both of you are wrong," he said. "Anybody who knows anything can see that this elephant is like a snake."

The fourth reached out his arms, and grasped one of the elephant's legs. "Oh, how blind you are!" he said. "It is very plain to me that he is round and tall like a tree."

The fifth was a very tall man, and he chanced to take hold of the elephant's ear. "The blindest man ought to know that this beast is not like any of the things that you name," he said.

"He is exactly like a huge fan."

The sixth was very blind indeed, and it was some time before he could find the elephant at all. At last he seized the animal's tail. "O foolish fellows!" he cried. "You surely have lost your senses. This elephant is not like a wall, or a spear, or a snake, or a tree; neither is he like a fan. But any man

with a particle of sense can see that he is exactly like a rope."

Then the elephant moved on, and the six blind men sat by the roadside all day, and quarreled about him. Each believed that he knew just how

The Fear of Tiptipwa

Once upon a time, there lived an old woman in a forest. She possessed a horse which she loved like her son. Grazing on the lush green grass in the forest, the horse had become healthy and robust.

The woman would tie it to a post under a banyan tree near her hut and massage its back and limbs before going to sleep at night.

The horse got sumptuous food and love every day and the woman had a companion in the desolate forest. One day, a thief saw the horse and decided to steal it. A tiger, too, came to know about the horse living under the woman's patronage and thought of feeding on it. Though the thief and the tiger had a common cause, they were unknown to each other and were unaware of each other's plan.

The weather changed abruptly the next day. A stormy blanket of cloud shrouded the forest after sunset. Flashes of lightning ripped through the inky atmosphere.

The horse was sitting near the hut where the woman was holed up.

The thief and the tiger found the scary weather appropriate to operate in. They stealthily reached the hut at the same time although separately. They prepared to strike the horse from two separate corners in opposite directions.

Though the tiger and the thief hadn't seen each other, the woman had sensed the presence of the enemies around.

Having lived in the jungle for years, the old woman had learnt how to deal with inclement weather and predators. Silently resting in her hut, she was cognizant of her horse's safety and security.

The tiger and the thief were focused on their prey. They were waiting for a brilliant flash of lightning to rip through the dark before they made their move. Suddenly, the old woman chanted in a loud voice, 'Neither do I fear a tiger nor a thief. What I am actually frightened of is Tiptipwa.'

The tiger and the thief got confused when they heard the woman's chant. They got distracted from their prey. 'What is Tiptipwa? The woman fears Tiptipwa more than me. This means that Tiptipwa is either a more dreaded animal than me or a monster or a ghost,' the tiger mused. The thief, on the other hand, thought that Tiptipwa might be some dangerous species and got frightened.

Just then, lightning forked through the graphite night, enabling the tiger and the thief to see the horse and strike. The tiger jumped on the horse. Simultaneously, the thief

threw a strap aiming at the neck of the horse. But instead, the strap fell around the neck of the tiger that had jumped on the horse.

The tiger, full of doubt about Tiptipwa, thought that it was Tiptipwa that had entrapped him. He got scared. The night had gotten inky again and nothing was visible in the darkness. Meanwhile, the thief thought that he had entrapped the horse. Thinking that the tiger was the horse, he mounted it. When the thief tried to climb it, the tiger thought that it was Tiptipwa that had overpowered him and tried to break free. When lightning struck again, the thief saw that he was sitting on the tiger and dismounted hurriedly. He

entered a hole in a tree to save himself.

The tiger ran and kept running till dawn broke. When a jackal saw the tiger running, he asked, 'O uncle! Why are you so nervous? You are our master. If you get so frightened, what will happen to us?'

The tiger paused, saying, 'O jackal! Tiptipwa had attacked me. He spared me only a little while ago and is hiding in that tree.' The jackal quipped, 'Don't worry, my master. Let us go together to get Tiptipwa out of the hole. We should kill and feast on him.'

The tiger and the jackal reached the tree in which the thief was holed up. The tiger asked the jackal to put his tail in the tree's hole to scare Tiptipwa out. But as the jackal moved his tail, the thief caught it and began pulling it with both his hands.

The jackal asked the tiger to shove his paw into the hole to scare Tiptipwa so that he would loosen his grip on the tail. But the tiger who was already scared fled. The

thief eventually pulled out the jackal's tail from his body. Wounded and stripped of his tail the jackal loitered in the forest pitiably for days. With time, his wounds healed but he was the subject of ridicule in his community. After many days, he was blessed with happiness when a she-jackal fell in love with him and they got married.

They bore five cubs after some time. Having lived together for long, the she-jackal asked her husband to take her to his home. The jackal took his wife and kids to a tunnel in the hills and described it as his home to his family.

As the she-jackal entered the burrow, she encountered an unusual smell.

'The burrow is filled with the smell of tigers. How can it be your home?' she asked her husband.

The jackal shot back, 'Honey, it is the smell of the tigers' meat. I hunt the tigers and eat their meat.'

Soon after they settled in the burrow, the jackal saw a tiger approaching them. It was the same tiger for whom the jackal had lost his tail.

The jackal got scared and revealed the truth to his wife.

But the she-jackal was cleverer.

She proposed, 'I will beat up the children, making them weep loudly. I will say that the kids are weeping for tiger's flesh. You should then ask the kids to stop making noise so that the tiger does not run away.'

The she-jackal beat up her children, making them cry, and the jackal asked them to keep quiet so that the tiger wouldn't run away—just like they had planned.

'The cubs are weeping for my meat! It might be another ploy of Tiptipwa to trap me,' the tiger thought and fled.

On his way, he encountered another jackal who said, 'Don't worry. The jackals who have occupied your home are my family friends. I will get them to vacate your den.'

The scared tiger tied the jackal to his hind legs and went to the burrow dragging him along. As the jackals in the burrow saw the tiger coming with another jackal, the she-jackal suggested to her husband, 'You should get angry at the jackal and say, "I had paid you to bring five tigers but you have brought only one. I won't spare you."'

The jackal did exactly that. The petrified tiger fled again, dragging the jackal with him. On the other hand, the jackal that had been stripped of his tail, lived happily with his family thereafter.

Fur and Feathers

Once upon a time, there was a mama Ostrich who lived in a forest by a village. One sunny morning, her eggs hatched in her nest and two little chicks were born. Mama Ostrich gleamed with happiness when she looked at her chicks and named them Pride and Joy. She went to gather food for her little ones from the village every day. Pride and Joy snuggled in her arms when she returned and fed them.

One day, when Mama Ostrich returned with the food, she was not able to find her two little chicks. She found footprints of wide paws around her nest and was certain that it was the king of the jungle who took her chicks away from her nest. She was alarmed.

Yet, she mustered the courage to get her little ones back and went to the lion's den. When she arrived at the den, she saw Pride and Joy resting on the furry arms of the lion. She was scared that the lion might harm them. She gathered herself and asked the lion to return her chicks.

The lion was not very happy to see Mama Ostrich at his den. He replied to her that Pride and Joy were his cubs and he would not give them away. As Mama Ostrich reasoned with the lion, he asked her to get any animal from the rest of the forest who would agree with her.

She went to the bear, giraffe, antelopes, zebras, and flamingoes, but every animal was scared to speak the truth in front of the lion. At last, the tired Mama Ostrich went to the mongoose and narrated her story.

The mongoose was very clever and he decided to find a way to help his friend. He had a great idea for the Ostrich and planned with her to dig a hole that led to the lion's den beneath the anthill.

Mama Ostrich had asked all the animals of the forest to gather at the anthill outside the lion's den.

When the animals gathered, the lion came out of his den with Pride and Joy, the two little chicks. Mama Ostrich told her story in front of the animals assembled there. She went to each animal and asked them to speak the truth and tell the lion that Pride and Joy were her little chicks. However, no one was ready for it. When she asked the Mongoose, he took a close glance at the little chicks, and said, "Have any of you ever seen a mama with fur having babies with feathers? These two little chicks have feathers on their body, whereas the lion has fur on his body. Pride and Joy belong to my friend, Ostrich!"

The lion was angry and growled and jumped at the mongoose. The mongoose jumped into the hole in the anthill and disappeared. The two little chicks walked to their mother and snuggled together. The lion was not aware of the other exit through the hole. He waited at the anthill for the mongoose to come out of the hole.

And his wait never ended. Mama Ostrich took her little chicks, Pride and Joy, to her nest and lived happily.

The Talking Fish

One day, while performing daily chores, a poor worker got a new job as a fisherman's helper. By his work, he was paid a few fish a day that managed the survival of him and his wife. What happened one day was this worker caught a pretty little fish. As he saw this fish, he was shocked to see a marvellous fish, and suddenly, the fish spoke to him in a human voice.

"See here, brother! Some time ago, I was playing with my friends, and I got caught in your net. Now I'm suffering and probably dying! My parents and my playmates must be looking for me and very anxious about my well being". Now the talking fish was gasping. Please show humanity and throw me back into the water!"

The worker started wondering and thought, could it be true? Was it possible that a fish lives a life filled with joys and sorrows, just like us? He quickly threw the fish back into the water. "All right, my pretty little fish, you are free to go along and play again- I don't want your parents and friends to worry for you anymore!"

When the worker's fisherman saw this, he got very angry.

"You idiot!" he yelled to the employee. "I hired you to capture fish, not to throw them back into the water! You're a worthless fool! Begone with you - I do not ever want to see you again!"

And the poor worker walked lamentably home. "What shall I tell my wife?" he wailed, dreading what would happen to them without his job.

He was walking alongside the street plunged in his sad thoughts, while all at once he noticed a Monster in human form coming toward him. The Monster was driving a very fine cow before him.

"Good day, brother," stated the Monster. "Why do you seem so sad?"

The worker conveyed the story to him.

"See here, my friend," stated the Monster. "I'm going to do you a favour. Do you see this cow? I'll let you preserve her for 3 years. She'll come up with plenty of good milk each day, and also you and your spouse will never go hungry. But you should keep this condition in mind: When 3 years have passed, I will come and ask certain questions of you. If you answer them correctly, the cow will be yours. But in case you do not, then I'll take each of you along with the cow, and do something I want with you. So, do you accept it?"

The worker thought, "I assume it is better to take the cow now than to head hungry. At least we're going to be able to sell the milk and stay for 3 years, after which we'll see what happens.

May be we're going to be fortunate enough to reply to those questions." So he accepted the terms, took the cow, and went home relieved and happy.

Indeed, the cow gave lots of good milk, sufficient for the worker and his spouse to drink and to sell, and in this way, provided the necessities of life.

In the evenings, the worker and his spouse might often sit collectively at their door, thinking about the Monster. They tried to think about what the solutions would possibly be. But as they'd no clue about what kind of questions the Monster might ask, they would always quit their sessions with a sigh and go to bed with bothered hearts. Day by day, the end of the 3 years grew closer and closer.

One evening, a good-looking youth came up to them.

"Good evening!" he stated. "I am so tired, and it's getting dark. If you please, may I also spend the night under your roof?"

"Of course, you may, but you should know that something horrible is going to happen to us tonight! Three years ago, we took a cow from a Monster. He informed us we could preserve the cow for 3 years, however, at the end of that time, he could come and ask us a few questions. If we solve the questions correctly, then the cow will be ours to keep, however, if we can't then we will become his prisoners forever. So in case you live us tonight, be cautious that no harm comes to you!"

"I see," stated the youth.

"Well, if it's alright with you, I'd just as soon stay the night." And so he did. Exactly at midnight, a knock was heard on the door. "Who's there?"

"It is I, the Monster! Three years have passed. The time has come to answer my questions!"

"We'll by no means be able to answer them!" wailed the poor worker and his spouse, clutching at each other's shoulders.

Suddenly, the youth stepped toward the door. He said to them, "Don't worry, I'll answer for you."

"I'm right here, waiting!" growled the Monster outside.

"And I'm right here also," replied the youth behind the door.

"Very well, then," stated the monster. "Where are you from?"

"I'm from the other side of the sea."

"How did you get right here?"

"Riding a lame flea!"

"Then the sea must have been very small?"

"Not at all. Even an eagle could not fly through it!"

"Then that eagle must have been a fledgling?"

"Not at all. The shadow of his wings would cover a whole town!"

"Then the town must have been very small?"

"Not at all. A hare could not run from one end to the other."

The Monster was speechless. It did not recognize what different questions to ask. He stood there silently at the door for some time, then disappeared into the darkness.

The poor worker and his spouse were overjoyed. They and the youth celebrated till dawn.

When sunrise was breaking, the youth said it was time for him to take his leave.

"Oh, no, we can't let you go!" cried the couple. "You saved our lives. Tell us what we can do to thank you." "You don't need to thank me," answered the youth. "I need to be on my way." "At least inform us who you are!" begged the worker.

"If you must know," stated the youth, "A kindness is never lost, even if you throw it into the water. I am that little talking fish which you threw back into the sea!"

Having said those words, he disappeared.